"If you desire to live your life the way it was meant to be lived – victoriously through Christ Jesus – then *The Journey: The Road to Empowerment* is a must read. TaRae Peoples grabs us and invites us to see ourselves in the real-life, often gut-wrenching experiences of women in the Bible. Their wounds, betrayals, triumphs and victories through Christ are our own – they are us. Reading and applying their stories to our lives is deeply transformational. Now, if you are looking to be coddled and told, 'It's okay honey, stay in your dysfunction. You poor little thing;' then do not read this book! The author expects something of you, expects you to acknowledge and surrender your own wrong thinking to God. She expects you to do some 'inside work' – taking responsibility, relinquishing bitterness, allowing the Holy Spirit to have His way in your heart. It's not easy, but you will feel like you do have a good friend, lovingly walking you through the process to wholeness as you read The Journey and as you allow the truths of scripture come alive in your own life. Let God use this book to push you along, to empower you to change for real and to live your life the way it was meant to be lived – victoriously through Jesus Christ. This just might be the book you have been waiting for!"

Pastor Kristen Gray, *Great Door Ministries*, **Omaha, NE**

The Journey

The Road to Empowerment

By
TaRae Peoples

The Journey
Copyright © 2014
TaRae Peoples

Cover design by Olivia Fries,
http://creativecenter.edu/portfolios/Fries_Olivia/

All rights reserved. No part of this publication may be reproduced, stored in a retrieval system, or transmitted in any form or by any means—electronic, mechanical, photocopying, recording, or otherwise—without the prior written permission of the publisher and copyright owner. The only exception is brief quotations in printed reviews.

SpiriTruth Publishing Company
Your multi-platform publishing partner
7710-T Cherry Park Drive, Suite 224
Houston, Texas 77095
www.WorldwidePublishingGroup.com
(713) 766-4272

Printed in the United States of America

EBook: 978-1-304-98904-8
Softcover: 978-1-365-73860-9

Contents

FOREWORD 7

THE PURPOSE 9

EMPOWERMENT 11

INTRODUCTION 13

CHAPTER 1 LEAH: SELF-ESTEEM 15

CHAPTER 2 TAMAR: NO LONGER THE VICTIM 39

CHAPTER 3 THE FORGIVEN WOMAN: I'M FORGIVEN 65

CHAPTER 4 GOMER: MY PAST IS NOT MY FUTURE 89

CHAPTER 5 THE ACCUSED WOMAN: DON'T REHEARSE YOUR MISTAKES ... 101

CHAPTER 6 RUTH: MOVING FORWARD 115

Foreword

I have been honored to sit under, and to experience the anointed worship leading of TaRae Peoples for more than five years at *Eagle's Nest Worship Center*, in Omaha Nebraska. TaRae sings with an anointing that pierces the darkness and cleanses the atmosphere.

Week after week she provides vocal avenues and harmonized opportunities in worship that usher in the presence of God. These worship sets focus the minds of the congregants on Jesus, and open their hearts to the teaching of God's Word.

Even when going through personal tragedy, TaRae has maintained her posture as a woman of God who knows in whom she believes, who abides in His righteousness, and who perseveres when it seems like all the hosts of the enemy's camp are attacking.

She and her husband Fred stand on the Word of God. This book is biblically-based, and if you follow the principles TaRae presents here you too will stand on God's Word.

I wasn't surprised to read her manuscript and see that the worship-leading anointing that rests on her life is also released in her writing. It too will usher you into the presence of God as you read this book. *Real freedom* can be found within these pages.

TaRae is the real deal. She has not just pulled together some Bible stories to write a book. She has relinquished the controls of her life to God in a disarming way, to format her and several biblical stories to help you unfold, unfurl, and unchain yourself from past mistakes, past hindrances, and past invasions.

Take TaRae's biblical examples plus her personal encouragement, practice them, and position yourself for success. You will be equipped to overcome in areas of your life that you could barely navigate previously. Blockages and hindrances that have pulled you downward will dissipate.

From this collection of stories, TaRae will pull practical advice and suggestions that will equip you to face your giants head-on, defeat them, and initiate new positive paths of freedom that you may have thought were impossible before. Congratulations for starting your journey by securing your copy of this book. You are now on track to arise from the debris of your past, and experience the love, joy, peace, and purpose of the abundant life Christ has promised you.

This could be the beginning of your greatest hour as God, the Author of your faith, authorizes and enables you to live as *a champion*.

Pastor Jay W. West
Anointed 2 Go Multi-denominational Ministries
Bellevue, NE

The Purpose

The purpose of this book is to prepare you for, and to encourage you in, life's difficult moments. The best person to encourage someone who is walking through a less than ideal situation is often one who has had to walk through the same or a similar situation. When I'm facing a difficult circumstance and need encouragement, I prefer to hear from someone who has experienced what I'm experiencing.

I have walked out every process I describe in this empowerment book. My words come from a place of compassion and understanding. Here you will have opportunities to make positive choices to help transform your future. My prayer is that you will uncover destiny, and your life will be changed!

Sincerely,
TaRae D. Peoples

Empowerment

Empowerment starts with you. You are the one who will decide to take whatever roads you travel in life. Since you are reading this, I assume that you desire to travel the road of life that is filled with greatness, peace, and joy.

To empower someone is to equip or enable them. You are now joining a family of women who have made the same decision you are making today. During this empowerment journey, you will be equipped with the right tools to enable you to be a successful woman.

Empowerment removes all excuses and reasons why you can't succeed. So today, your new life statement begins with *I can*!

- *I can* be all God has called, and desires for me to be.
- *I can* accomplish all of my God-given dreams.
- *I can* be a woman of excellence and of high esteem.
- *I can* go further than I've ever imagined.

"I can do all things through Christ who strengthens me" (Philippians 4:13).

Along this road, detours will be taken; construction zones will be encountered; but, you're not traveling this road alone. You are *never alone*.

Based on the empowerment reading thus far, how do you see yourself now, and how would you like to see yourself at the end of this journey?

_____
_____
_____
_____
_____
_____
_____
_____
_____
_____
_____
_____
_____
_____
_____
_____
_____
_____

Introduction

It's amazing how some women can walk through the majority of their lives bound, never to experience true freedom. Even more astounding is that most of those women don't even know they are bound. They mask their bondage with statements like:

- "I'm not mean, I'm guarded," which translates; "I don't know how to trust you."
- "That's just the way I was raised." What you really mean is "I don't want to change."
- "I just don't have time for that," but what you are truly saying is: "I don't want you to see the real me."

Declarations like these may sound noble and mature, but in reality they hold many of us in a box that prevents us from dealing with the real issues.

For the majority of us, these bondages were placed on us by lies spoken over us by family, supposed friends, and other random people. However, there is hope! There is a three-point system of operation we can follow which will enable us to be set free!

1. *We Must Acknowledge.* We have to be honest and transparent with ourselves over things that hinder us. No one knows us like we know ourselves. Only we know what is hidden in the darkest places of our hearts. So, let's go in and take authority over it.

2. *We Must Ask.* We must be willing to ask for help. Lies like, "no one understands," or "I am the only one who is dealing with these things," are the kinds of lies Satan wants us to embrace.

3. *We Must Announce.* God's announcement of who He has called us to be is our "all access all-expense paid trip to freedom!" When we speak what God speaks, we're speaking the perfect and complete will of God over our lives. Why would we choose to speak anything less than that which is perfect? God has outlined our destiny and future, but it is up to us to step into it and produce fruit from the seeds of greatness He has planted inside us.

   In this book we can journey out of bondage and into freedom. Along the way, we will *acknowledge* our mistakes. Let's *ask* God to help us maneuver past them and *announce* our future!

   On your mark, get set, GROW!

Chapter 1

Leah: Self-Esteem

Scripture Reference: Genesis 29 (NKJV,)
Jacob Meets Rachel

So Jacob went on his journey and came to the land of the people of the East. ² And he looked, and saw a well in the field; and behold, there were three flocks of sheep lying by it; for out of that well they watered the flocks. A large stone was on the well's mouth. ³ Now all the flocks would be gathered there; and they would roll the stone from the well's mouth, water the sheep, and put the stone back in its place on the well's mouth. ⁴ And Jacob said to them, "My brethren, where are you from?" And they said, "We are from Haran." ⁵ Then he said to them, "Do you know Laban the son of Nahor?" And they said, "We know him." ⁶ So he said to them, "Is he well?" And they said, "He is well. And look, his daughter Rachel is coming with the sheep." ⁷ Then he said, "Look, it is still high day; it is not time for the cattle to be gathered together. Water the sheep, and go and feed them." ⁸ But they said, "We cannot until all the flocks are gathered together, and they have rolled the stone from the well's mouth; then we water the sheep." ⁹ Now while he was still speaking with them, Rachel came with her father's sheep, for she was a shepherdess. ¹⁰ And it came to pass, when Jacob saw Rachel the daughter of Laban his mother's brother, and the sheep of Laban his mother's brother, that Jacob went near and rolled the stone from the well's mouth, and watered the flock of Laban his mother's brother. ¹¹ Then Jacob kissed Rachel, and lifted up his voice and wept. ¹² And Jacob told Rachel that he was her father's relative and that he was Rebekah's son. So she ran and told her father. ¹³ Then it came to pass, when Laban heard the report about Jacob his sister's son, that he ran to meet him, and embraced him and kissed him, and brought him to his house. So he told Laban all these things. ¹⁴ And Laban said to him, "Surely you are my bone and my flesh." And he stayed with him for a month.

Jacob Marries Leah and Rachel

¹⁵ Then Laban said to Jacob, "Because you are my relative, should you therefore serve me for nothing? Tell me, what should your wages be?" ¹⁶ Now Laban had two daughters: the name of the elder was Leah, and the name of the younger was Rachel. ¹⁷ Leah's eyes were delicate, but Rachel was beautiful of form and appearance. ¹⁸ Now Jacob loved Rachel; so he said, "I will serve you seven years for Rachel your younger daughter." ¹⁹ And Laban said, "It is better that I give her to you than that I should give her to another man. Stay with me." ²⁰ So Jacob served seven years for Rachel, and they seemed only a few days to him because of the love he had for her. ²¹ Then Jacob said to Laban, "Give me my wife, for my days are fulfilled, that I may go in to her." ²² And Laban gathered together all the men of the place and made a feast. ²³ Now it came to pass in the evening that he took Leah his daughter and brought her to Jacob; and he went in to her. ²⁴ And Laban gave his maid Zilpah to his daughter Leah as a maid. ²⁵ So it came to pass in the morning, that behold, it was Leah. And he said to Laban, "What is this you have done to me? Was it not for Rachel that I served you? Why then have you deceived me?" ²⁶ And Laban said, "It must not be done so in our country, to give the younger before the firstborn. ²⁷ Fulfill her week, and we will give you this one also for the service which you will serve with me still another seven years." ²⁸ Then Jacob did so and fulfilled her week. So he gave him his daughter Rachel as wife also. ²⁹ *And Laban gave his maid Bilhah to his daughter Rachel as a maid.* ³⁰ *Then Jacob also went in to Rachel, and he also loved Rachel more than Leah. And he served with Laban still another seven years.*

The Children of Jacob

³¹ *When the* LORD *saw that Leah was unloved, He opened her womb; but Rachel was barren.* ³² *So Leah conceived and bore a son, and she called his name Reuben; for she said, "The* LORD *has surely looked on my affliction. Now therefore, my husband will love me."* ³³ *Then she conceived again and bore a son, and said, "Because the* LORD *has heard that I am unloved, He has therefore given me this son also." And she called his name Simeon.* ³⁴ *She conceived again and bore a son, and said, "Now this time my husband will become attached to me, because I have borne him three sons." Therefore his name was called Levi.*[c] ³⁵ *And she conceived again and bore a son, and said, "Now I will praise the* LORD.*" Therefore she called his name Judah. Then she stopped bearing.*

It's a love story of a family being reconciled after many years apart. It's also a story of deception and scheming. We are being guided through the life of a woman who's being thrown into the circle of lies that sets the course for her life.

In reading this biblical account, we discover a lot about most of the characters in this story.

Let's see: Jacob has run away from his hometown to escape the wrath of his having stolen his brother's birthright.

Laban is a man of means and influence. Both he and Jacob are well known in the city.

Rachel is described as beautiful of form and appearance. She's a shepherdess, a position of responsibility in her father's house, and she also is well-known. How do we know that? The men who greeted Jacob upon his arrival told him who she was.

Then there's Leah. The only description we have for her in this story is that she is Rachel's elder sister and her eyes were delicate. Or to be blunt, Leah was unattractive. There is no mention of her occupation or her status in the community. There already seems to be some major imbalance here.

When most ministers reference this story, they mention how much Jacob loved Rachel and how unfairly Laban treated him. They stress how Jacob was forced to endure seven years of labor while desiring Rachel every day, and how horrible it was for Laban to do such a thing to Jacob.

Well, I beg to differ. Jacob brought the idea of his waiting seven years upon himself. Instead of our focusing on how unfair life was for Jacob, how about we consider how unfair those seven years were to Leah? She was used as a pawn in the scheme between these two men. Neither of them had her best interest at heart, nor considered how their actions would affect her.

Leah wakes up one morning to discover she is getting married. Not only is she getting married, but she's getting married to the man who has worked seven years *to get her sister*.

Her father throws a party to celebrate this union and officially gives her away. Leah's wedding night comes and her new husband tells her all the right things. He woos and caresses her, and whispers sweet nothings to her. This was the greatest night of her life. Undoubtedly Jacob tells her how beautiful she is, thinking he was talking to Rachel, which could have been the first time Leah's ever heard herself referred to in such a desirable manner. However, she wakes up the next morning and finds the man who spoke so gently to her the night before, bitter, disappointed, and infuriated because she is not the woman he wants and bargained for.

This story, with a few variations, describes so many of us. We get involved in these relationships based on pretense only to have the rug pulled out from under us. Sometimes the pretense comes from what we hoped would happen in a relationship. The majority of the time it's based on a figment of our imagination. In turn, we become devastatingly disappointed when things don't turn out the way we imagined they would. We rarely recognize the real picture. As a result, we allow ourselves to walk into situations without having all the *right* information.

Referring back to our story, Leah is preparing to become someone's wife. I'm sure she had a feeling that something wasn't exactly right. However, nowhere does it say that Leah wondered about, or asked any questions regarding her future husband. She simply showed up dressed for her wedding, said her vows, and fulfilled her wifely duty. Many of us, if we are honest, will admit to having acted in similar fashion.

We had reservations about the situation, yet we asked few if any probing questions. We ignored our God-given intuition, the flashing red light, the ear piercing bullhorn, the screaming voice in our head that yelled, "STOP! YOU'RE GOING THE WRONG WAY!" Rarely do we guard ourselves, err on the side of caution, and say, "Better safe than sorry."

Instead, we blindly and foolishly enter into relationships with the wrong men. Or we become friends with someone and tell them too much of our business. We often assume that everyone is good, and they only want what's best for us. We throw caution to the wind, and sacrifice ourselves in the process.

As a result of entering into these toxic relationships, our self-esteem becomes distorted, suppressed, and produces a negative self-image which we perceive as normal. Why? We do this partly because the wrong people have spoken into and over our lives.

Choosing the right circle of influence is a vital life survival tactic. Without it, life will leave us empty and lonely. Being surrounded by the right influential people will make a drastic difference in our lives, and we will begin to focus on new outcomes.

Let's look at Mary, the mother of Jesus, for a moment. When she was carrying God's promised Messiah she left home, and went to her cousin's house. She decided to remove herself from people and surroundings that did not speak favorably of "The Promise." The Bible says, "She made haste," which means she left in a hurry.

We can learn a lot from Mary's swift action. We can admit to holding on to old ways of living and doing things because they are comfortable, but what if Mary had done that? Instead of being comfortable, Mary told God, *"Be it unto me, just as you have said."* She put her faith into action and moved towards a place where her gift could be developed. She didn't wait for anyone. She didn't talk herself out of "The Promise." Too many of us wait around for other people to go with us, and those we are waiting on are not equipped to go where we are headed.

Mary connected with Elizabeth who understood the stress of being the topic of public scrutiny. Elizabeth was pregnant with her own promise (her baby would be John the Baptist). She understood Mary's desire to fulfill God's work.

In our story, Leah has no such connection. The story makes no reference to Leah's mother, and now the only other woman-to-woman relationship she has, is scared because of her father's scheme. There is seemingly no place for Leah to find refuge. It's safe to say that, like so many of us, Leah was willing to try to create this picture of a family, to take the edge off of feeling alone and isolated. She entered a marriage, even if it meant being connected to someone who didn't really love her.

Reader, this may rings true for you right now. Maybe some of the influential woman-to-woman relationships in your life are stressed, not the best, and you're feeling alone. I'm here to encourage and reassure you that you are not alone. God sent me to tell you that He's still with you! You are precious to Him, and He wants only the best for you.

Hebrews 13:5 says, "...*For He Himself has said 'I will never leave you nor forsake you.'*"

By failing to evaluate what was happening, Leah finds herself in a love-less marriage, and in an estranged relationship with her sister. She tries to gain the attention, admiration, and affection of a man who doesn't want her. She is wearing herself out trying to catch and keep his attention.

Leah gives birth to one son, and she says, "My husband will see me."

She has another son and responds this time, "Now my husband will hear me."

She has a third son and suggests, "Finally, my husband will be joined to me."

Leah was not the desired, or the more prominent sibling, so I'm sure she is quite familiar with trying to get people to notice her.

If you reflect back over your life, you too can pinpoint times when you worked to get someone's attention. You may not have to think back too far. That might even be where you find yourself today. Maybe your attention seeking tactics have caused you to dress a certain way, hoping to gain the attention of a young man thinking; *now he will call me.*

If not that, perhaps you thought *if I go to the party, then she will be my friend.* Or, *if I join this Bible study group, then I will be considered part of the group.* You are too valuable to have to compromise yourself to get anyone's attention. If you find yourself pretending to enjoy certain things, or find yourself agreeing with someone so you will fit in, (yes, adult women still do this), then I'm speaking to you.

Now Leah is expecting again. But something is different this time. She gives Jacob a fourth son, names him "Judah," and says, "Now I will praise the Lord!" The Bible then declares in Genesis 29:35, "*...she stopped bearing.*" Leah stopped bearing because she came to realize that Jacob could never be the source of her happiness.

Leah learns a valuable lesson that we often forget. She honed in on *the power of praise.* Leah's in the middle of the most uncomfortable and confining moment in her life married to a man who loves only her sister, and not her. Her father is using her for his own selfish gain, and her children are watching her maneuver through this difficulty. The lesson she teaches us is that even in the most uncomfortable and trying times, we must not forget to praise.

1 Thessalonians 5:18 says, "*In **everything** give thanks, for this is the will of God in Christ Jesus for you.*" Praise releases supernatural energy that changes the atmosphere. Praise produces peace that invades your natural circumstance. Philippians 4:6-7 encourages us, in whatever situation we

find ourselves, to *"be anxious for nothing, but in everything by prayer and supplication, with **thanksgiving**, let your requests be made known to God; and the peace of God, which surpasses all understanding, will guard your hearts and minds through Christ Jesus."*

Praise transforms our thoughts, and redirects our focus. We begin to feel better physically, and gain emotional stability. We will no longer be on edge, ready to fall to pieces, because in the midst of our praise we are no longer looking at what is wrong in the natural. Instead, we are focused on the goodness and greatness of our God. This heavenly focus brings us up higher, clarifies our vision, and helps us look past our pain to see the big picture.

In Leah's case, at the beginning of her marriage, God used her children as a sign of His love for her. The Bible says in Genesis 29:1, *"When the Lord saw that Leah was unloved, He opened her womb..."* God took notice of Leah's situation, which should encourage us. No matter where we are, or what we face, God sees us, and has plans for us!

God's opening Leah's womb, and allowing her to bear children, made her position known. In those days, bearing a son was expected of a woman. God allowed her to give birth to *four sons*. True, Jacob didn't notice her, but God did. And at the birth of Judah, Leah wisely decided to focus on God's faithfulness, rather than Jacob's neglect.

After discovering she was incapable of fixing the situation, Leah ran to the arms of the only One who could help. To depend on ourselves to fix life's problems is a mistake. We cannot bring completeness into our lives because we are human. And being human leaves room for error. Therefore, any fix we come up with will be flawed.

Trying to be satisfied with the admiration and acceptance of others is fleeting and disappointing. People's opinions of us can change as easily as the changing patterns of the waves on the seashore. These may be prominent people in our lives, and we may admire their accomplishments, but they cannot assure us of joy or happiness. True joy and happiness is found in the presence of the Lord. Psalm 16:11 says, *"You will show me the path of life; in Your presence is fullness of joy; At Your right hand are pleasures forevermore."*

Entering into the presence of the Lord isn't hard and doesn't take hours to accomplish. It is as simple as thinking about Him. The moment we set our minds on the Lord, He shows up. Taking out time to talk to Him and acknowledge His presence brings us clarity throughout our day. The unimportant events, that we used to give our time and attention to, become irrelevant. Because we've been in the presence of the Lord, those things that once upset us, and got us bent out of shape, don't grab our attention anymore.

The more we practice entering His presence, the more we'll see Him in our lives. Even in the things we take for granted. We will see Him in the sunrise and sunset. We'll see his creativity in the shapes of the clouds, and in the colors of the sky. We'll appreciate the beauty of the trees, and the sounds of the birds. We'll become awestruck at the sight of the movement of the waters, and the creatures that live in them.

While Leah was carrying Judah she had a special encounter with God. She noticed all the blessings He had given her, and recognized He was preparing to do it again. When she saw the beautiful gift God gave her, a fourth son, because she had found her place of joy and happiness in His presence, she continued to praise God! After giving birth to Judah, the Bible says in Genesis 29:35, *"Leah stopped bearing."* Leah had graduated from needing the approval of a man to being confident that she had the attention of God!

I recall times in my life where I would share what seemed to be all my business with anyone who showed an interest. I was desperate to be accepted. My thought was, *perhaps if I share something I won't feel so isolated and will finally be accepted.* What I didn't realize was that *I was already accepted.* Our acceptance is settled! Ephesians 1:6 teaches us, *"...to the praise of the glory of His grace, by which He made us accepted in the Beloved."*

The Bible says *"Leah's eyes were delicate (weak, lazy), but Rachel (her sister) was beautiful of form and appearance."* These two statements are pretty extreme. Two sisters have been compared, and one is obviously winning over the other. It goes on to describe the story of a man who was tricked into marrying the undesired sister. Not only was her father using her for his purposes, she was left to live with a husband who didn't love her, and didn't want her. How much self-esteem do you think she had?

When has your self-esteem been tested by the opinions of others? And what effect did that have on your life?

_____
_____
_____
_____
_____
_____
_____
_____

Leah didn't ask for this. She was neither flirting with Jacob to win his attention, nor taunting Rachel about being the oldest, and her having the birthright to be first to marry. It is safe to assume that Leah was very aware of the fact that she was not the most physically attractive, based on the standards of the time, and was okay with it.

Then she was forced to suffer the humiliation of being married to a man that seemed to adore her on their wedding night, but wanted nothing to do with her the next morning. Despite all of this, she was determined to be the best wife to Jacob that she could be. She created a home for him, and dutifully bore him three sons thinking that this would surely get his attention.

Describe a time when you wanted someone to see you (Reuben), to hear you (Simeon), to attach themselves to you, or want to be around you (Levi)?

_____
_____
_____
_____
_____
_____
_____

How do you think each one of Leah's relationships between, Laban, Jacob and Rachel shaped her self-image?

_____
_____

Who in your life or what situations in your life have helped shape and create your self-image? These could be positive or negative.

Leah decided to praise God even in the midst of chaos and changed her perception of herself and her circumstances. What perceptions of yourself do you want to change?

After realizing that all of her attempts to please Jacob by bearing him sons, cooking, and cleaning would neither get nor keep his attention, Leah turns to the only One who cares. She bears a fourth son, and names him Judah (which means praise). Then she stops bearing.

You see, this scenario was never about the character flaws of Laban, Jacob, or Rachel. This was always about Leah's misplaced focus. It took Leah seven years to focus her attention on God, and discover that He'd been there all along. It was then that she decided to praise Him.

Are you suffering from misplaced focus? Who or what have you given your focus to? And why?

What have you learned from Leah's response and how can her response help change things for you?

_____
_____
_____
_____
_____
_____
_____
_____

Praise is powerful! It's an atmosphere changer, and a spiritual climate adjuster. When we praise God, the Creator of the universe, the Ruler of heaven and earth, things change. The game is no longer the same. We have the advantage.

Labels Good and Bad

Because of our current situation, labels have become associated with us. They have not been good labels. These labels may be ones we've given ourselves; or maybe they have been placed on us by others. Regardless of the source, they ultimately help form our lives.

The word "label" means, a distinctive name or trademark that identifies a product. In this portion of our workbook, let's discuss some labels that have been placed on us. List a few of those labels.

_____
_____
_____
_____
_____
_____

Labels are considered good or bad based on their context. If we use words like silly or stupid to describe an individual, we are not building them up, we are tearing them down. These are labels with which we would rather not be associated. However, using a word such as successful to describe someone encourages them and gives them life. With that being said, what labels would you like to be associated with your name?

_____
_____
_____
_____
_____

Now that you have listed the words you want to be attached to your name, start using them to describe yourself. Your new self-descriptions should sound like this: *I am fearfully and wonderfully made! I am strong, intelligent and wise!* Begin to create your own and recite them daily. Doing this adjusts your own self-perception.

Empowerment Scriptures

"What then shall we say to these things? If God be for us, who can be against us" (Romans 8:31)?

"I will praise You, for I am fearfully and wonderfully made; Marvelous are Your works, and that my soul knows very well" (Psalm 139:14).

"Before I formed you in the womb I knew you; before you were born I sanctified you ..."
(Jeremiah 1:5a).

Our Self-Esteem Confession

I will praise You God for I am fearfully and wonderfully made. I am a marvelous work of your hand. Before I was formed in my mother's womb, you knew me. You set me apart before I was born. I can accomplish great things because you are for me. I will not be afraid of the faces of those who do not believe in me because you believe in me; therefore, I believe in me!

My Journal…

Chapter 2

Tamar: No Longer the Victim

Scripture Reference: 2 Samuel 13

Amnon and Tamar

> After this Absalom the son of David had a lovely sister, whose name was Tamar; and Amnon the son of David loved her. ² Amnon was so distressed over his sister Tamar that he became sick; for she was a virgin. And it was improper for Amnon to do anything to her. ³ But Amnon had a friend whose name was Jonadab the son of Shimeah, David's brother. Now Jonadab was a very crafty man. ⁴ And he said to him, "Why are you, the king's son, becoming thinner day after day? Will you not tell me?" Amnon said to him, "I love Tamar, my brother Absalom's sister." ⁵ So Jonadab said to him, "Lie down on your bed and pretend to be ill. And when your father comes to see you, say to him,

'Please let my sister Tamar come and give me food, and prepare the food in my sight, that I may see it and eat it from her hand.'" ⁶ *Then Amnon lay down and pretended to be ill; and when the king came to see him, Amnon said to the king, "Please let Tamar my sister come and make a couple of cakes for me in my sight, that I may eat from her hand." ⁷ And David sent home to Tamar, saying, "Now go to your brother Amnon's house, and prepare food for him." ⁸ So Tamar went to her brother Amnon's house; and he was lying down. Then she took flour and kneaded it, made cakes in his sight, and baked the cakes. ⁹ And she took the pan and placed them out before him, but he refused to eat. Then Amnon said, "Have everyone go out from me." And they all went out from him. ¹⁰ Then Amnon said to Tamar, "Bring the food into the bedroom, that I may eat from your hand." And Tamar took the cakes which she had made, and brought them to Amnon her brother in the bedroom. ¹¹ Now when she had brought them to him to eat, he took hold of her and said to her, "Come, lie with me, my sister." ¹² But she answered him, "No, my brother, do not force me, for no such thing should be done in Israel. Do not do this disgraceful thing! ¹³ And I, where could I take my shame? And as for you, you would be like*

one of the fools in Israel. Now therefore, please speak to the king; for he will not withhold me from you." ¹⁴ *However, he would not heed her voice; and being stronger than she, he forced her and lay with her.*

¹⁵ *Then Amnon hated her exceedingly, so that the hatred with which he hated her was greater than the love with which he had loved her. And Amnon said to her, "Arise, be gone!"* ¹⁶ *So she said to him, "No, indeed! This evil of sending me away is worse than the other that you did to me." But he would not listen to her.* ¹⁷ *Then he called his servant who attended him, and said, "Here! Put this woman out, away from me, and bolt the door behind her."* ¹⁸ *Now she had on a robe of many colors, for the king's virgin daughters wore such apparel. And his servant put her out and bolted the door behind her.* ¹⁹ *Then Tamar put ashes on her head, and tore her robe of many colors that was on her, and laid her hand on her head and went away crying bitterly.* ²⁰ *And Absalom her brother said to her, "Has Amnon your brother been with you? But now hold your peace, my sister. He is your brother; do not take this thing to heart." So Tamar remained desolate in her brother Absalom's house.* ²¹ *But when King David heard of all these things, he was very angry.* ²² *And Absalom spoke to his brother*

Amnon neither good nor bad. For Absalom hated Amnon, because he had forced his sister Tamar.

Absalom Murders Amnon

²³ And it came to pass, after two full years, that Absalom had sheepshearers in Baal Hazor, which is near Ephraim; so Absalom invited all the king's sons. ²⁴ Then Absalom came to the king and said, "Kindly note, your servant has sheepshearers; please, let the king and his servants go with your servant." ²⁵ But the king said to Absalom, "No, my son, let us not all go now, lest we be a burden to you." Then he urged him, but he would not go; and he blessed him. ²⁶ Then Absalom said, "If not, please let my brother Amnon go with us." And the king said to him, "Why should he go with you?" ²⁷ But Absalom urged him; so he let Amnon and all the king's sons go with him. ²⁸ Now Absalom had commanded his servants, saying, "Watch now, when Amnon's heart is merry with wine, and when I say to you, 'Strike Amnon!' then kill him. Do not be afraid. Have I not commanded you? Be courageous and valiant." ²⁹ So the servants of Absalom did to Amnon as Absalom had commanded. Then all the king's sons arose, and each one got on his mule and fled. ³⁰ And it came to pass, while they were on the way, that news came to David, saying, "Absalom has killed all the king's sons, and not one of them is left!" ³¹ *So the king arose and tore his garments and lay on the ground, and all his servants stood by with their clothes torn.* ³² *Then Jonadab the son of Shimeah, David's brother, answered and said, "Let not my lord suppose they have killed all the young men, the king's sons, for only Amnon is dead. For by the command of Absalom this has been determined from the day that he forced his sister Tamar.* ³³ *Now therefore, let not my lord the king take the thing to his heart, to think that all the king's sons are dead. For only Amnon is dead."*

Absalom Flees to Geshur

³⁴ *Then Absalom fled. And the young man who was keeping watch lifted his eyes and looked, and there, many people were coming from the road on the hillside behind him.* ³⁵ *And Jonadab said to the king, "Look, the king's sons are coming; as your servant said, so it is."* ³⁶ *So it was, as soon as he had finished speaking, that the king's sons indeed came, and they lifted up their voice and wept. Also the king and all his servants wept very bitterly.* ³⁷ *But Absalom fled and went to Talmai the son of Ammihud, king of*

Geshur. And David mourned for his son every day. *³⁸ So Absalom fled and went to Geshur, and was there three years. ³⁹ And King David longed to go to Absalom. For he had been comforted concerning Amnon, because he was dead.*

Our story of reference is that of Tamar and Amnon. Here is a well-meaning young woman who had all the right intentions of tending to the needs of someone she cared about, and in return she was seriously mistreated. Amnon was in love with Tamar, and truly desired her; however, he allowed the opinions of friends to cloud his judgment. This caused him great detriment in his family relationships, not to mention severed any genuine feelings between he and the woman he loved. Tamar gets thrown into the pot of deception and lustful thoughts; as a result Amnon suffers greatly from his actions.

How many times have you found yourself in a situation where your motives were right, only to have someone else's wrong intentions uncovered leaving you to pay for it?

You have no control over the thoughts, intentions, and misbehavior of others. However, you can control your response to their actions and immediately establish standards! In this chapter you will work the action steps described in the introduction.

Step One: Acknowledge

Acknowledge! Acknowledgment is not to accept as okay negative things that have happened to you. Nor is acknowledgment lying to yourself, saying, "it didn't happen," or "I can cover this up and no one will ever have to know." To acknowledge is to accept the truth or the existence of something, even if the truth is that some horrible and awful things have happened to you. But that does not mean you should allow them to define you!

In our story we see Tamar begging Amnon not to do this horrible thing to her because it would be disgraceful. Tamar knew that this one incident would be a defining moment in her life. The confidence she had prior to entering his (Amnon's) room was gone. The security that a young lady has when entering the house of a trusted relative had been stripped from her. A horrendous act was suddenly committed against her and she was left to walk alone, humiliated.

In verse 19 we read that Tamar put ashes on her head and tore the robe she wore that signified her virginity and cried. Everyone in that kingdom understood the significance of her robe. Her garment, which symbolized honor, respect, virtue, and high esteem, had been replaced with the defamation of her character. Those around her stared at her, mocked her, and gossiped about her. From that moment she began to live by a single event.

How many times have you stopped living according to *who you are*, and started living according to *what happened to you*?

Okay, so let's deal with the thoughts you may be having right now. You might be thinking, "I didn't do this horrible thing to myself. They lied about me. He left me. I was abused and mistreated." The list can go on and on. However, even if all of these thoughts are true, you can decide to be defined by the things that happened to you or by the purpose God has designed for you.

We empower the abuser every time we stop moving forward. Rehearsing the past and laying down your authority is a decision you make for yourself. No one has the power to take that from you. The Bible says:

"If God be for us, who can be against us" (Romans 8:31).

"Yet in all these things we are more than conquerors through Him who loved us" (Romans 8:37).

"Many are the afflictions of the righteous, but the Lord delivers him out of them all" (Psalm 34:19).

In each one of those verses the dominating factor is that God is involved. God is *for* us! God *loves* us! God *has delivered* us! These are guarantees established in the Word of God.

Many of us have been talked about and ridiculed because of the detours we've had to take. In some cases, that has caused us to focus on the negative and the lack of support so much, that we've completely ignored the positive that is being produced, and the support that we do have. We know first-hand what it means to be disregarded during what seems to be the most crucial moments in our lives.

Life has dealt with us cruelly, especially when it comes to suffering due to the misguided decisions of others. We are mistreated and then we're thrown away like we've done something wrong? One lesson I've learned is that the majority of the hurtful acts committed against me had nothing to do with me. They were evidence of massive character flaws of the person who hurt me.

Tamar has been raped by someone who should've guarded and protected her. Instead, he took something valuable from her, and then threw her away. The Bible says in 2 Samuel 13:15: *"Then Amnon hated her exceedingly, so that the hatred with which he hated her was greater than the love with which he had loved her. And Amnon said to her, Arise, be gone!"*

You may have been raped, beaten, maybe mentally and verbally abused. Or perhaps you've suffered the humiliation of being forced to drop out of school and return home to raise a child alone. Some are facing recovery from an addiction, a divorce, or the unexpected loss of a loved one. All of which are devastating at one point or another, and yes, you are allowed time to grieve and to hurt; but the blessing is *your negative life experiences need not determine your destiny.* DO NOT plant a flag there and build your life around that unfortunate event.

Yes it hurts and some days it seems unbearable, but God is still there with you. In 1 Peter 5:7 we read: *"casting all your care upon Him, for He cares for you."* Let this Scripture be a faithful reminder that God cares for you. There is nothing you have encountered that He is not concerned about. You are His! 1 John 4:4 NLT says: *"But you belong to God, my dear children. You have already won a victory over those people, because the Spirit who lives in you is greater than the spirit who lives in the world."*

What can we learn from Tamar? Let's go back to verse 19. There are many ways we can view this verse, but I want to address two of them. The first way we could look at it is the way I mentioned earlier. Don't allow your present circumstance to dictate how you live the rest of your life. Remember God's promise to you, Jeremiah 29:11: *"For I know the thoughts I think toward you, says the Lord, thoughts of peace and not of evil, to give you a future and a hope."*

The comfort in your *present* circumstance is that it is temporary. Your *present* is always changing. *Presently* you are reading this book, however, an hour from now your *present* maybe preparing dinner or studying for an exam. 2 Corinthians 4:18 says *"while we do not look at the things which are seen, but at the things which are not seen. <u>For the things which are seen are temporary</u>, but the things which are not seen are eternal."*

A second way to look at it is to not be embarrassed by your flaws, but use them as building tools. Tamar's immediate response to her unfortunate situation was to show the world her flaws. She was no longer "perfect." She had been through something horrific. In Revelation 12:11 we read, *"…they overcame him by the blood of the Lamb and by the word of their testimony…"* To expose your flaws to the world overcomes the enemy. For you to be transparent after having made a mistake is the last thing you want to do. However, when you hide, you allow the enemy to turn your mind into his personal playground. He will fill it with lies and, ***amplify*** any insecurity you have. But, when you admit your imperfections there is nothing for the enemy to use against you. They've already been revealed. Remember, broken people are all God has to work with!

- Every time you encourage someone with your testimony, you are overcoming the enemy.

- When you talk of the greatness of God and how faithful He's been to you, you overcome the enemy.
- As you thank God for the blessings He's bestowed upon you in the hard places of your life, you overcome the enemy.

If the enemy can keep you quiet you give him the advantage. You can take away his advantage by choosing to praise the Lord! Your praise neutralizes the enemy's attack. Look what God says...

1 Peter 5:8 NLT warns, *"Be alert! Watch out for your great enemy, the devil. He prowls around like a roaring lion, looking for someone to devour."*

Psalm 27:1 says, *"The Lord is my light and my salvation; whom shall I fear? The Lord is the strength of my life; whom shall I be afraid."*

Philippians 4:6-8 says, *"Be anxious for nothing, but in everything by prayer and supplication, with thanksgiving, let your requests be made known to God; and the peace of God, which surpasses all understanding, will guard your hearts and minds through Christ Jesus. Finally, brethren, whatever things are true, whatever things are noble, whatever things are just, whatever things are* pure, *whatever things are* lovely, *if there is any* virtue *and if there is anything* praiseworthy, <u>*meditate on these things*</u>."

As long as your mind is set on good things, or even better – as long as your mind is set on godly things, there's no room for the bad stuff. Colossians 3:2, AMP says, *"And set your minds and keep them set on what is above (the higher things), not on the things on the earth."*

So what does the enemy do? He plants a seed of embarrassment in your mind to cripple you from taking the first step, which is acknowledgment. Acknowledgment says "I already know this about myself and God does too." The intent of the enemy is to silence you regarding your past and your imperfections, forcing you to put on a façade. Trust me, image management is exhausting.

At this point, you must constantly appear perfect, and have the pressure of always keeping things in order. For people to see you without your mask is unacceptable because the real you is flawed and slightly damaged. But the devil is a liar! The Word of God clearly tells us that *"The thief does not come except to steal, and to kill and to destroy..."* (John 10:10). Your silence enables the enemy to steal your freedom. By keeping silent, you strengthen the chains that bind you. If you remain silent you lose!

Tamar didn't keep quiet. She ran out in her new identity to a place of safety. She ran to her brother who was all too willing to avenge his sister's honor. At this time you may be thinking "I don't have anyone to avenge my honor." That's another lie from the enemy. Christ avenged your honor on the cross. He settled it for you. *Accept it.*

The Word of God says in Romans 12:19, *"Beloved, do not avenge yourselves, but rather give place to wrath; for it is written, Vengeance is Mine, I will repay, says the Lord."* Tamar didn't have to repay Amnon for what he did to her, because there was already a plan in place to redeem her honor.

It's at these times that you decide to *"...cast all your care upon Him..."* The, Amplified Bible says in 1 Peter 5:7, *"Casting the whole of your care* [all your anxieties, all your worries, all your concerns, once and for all] *on Him, for He cares for you affectionately and cares about you watchfully."* That deserves a praise break right there!

Step Two: Ask

Ask! Now we are in a better position to ask God for help. Say this prayer out loud:

> *"Daddy, I need your help! I am drowning in my low self-image and victim mentality. I'm ready to come out. I am done doubting you! I am done*

wasting time! I am done living defeated! Thank you for helping me! In Jesus' name, Amen!"

Now take a minute to praise God for answering your prayer. Don't be ashamed to put this book down, lift your hands, throw your head back and really get one in! Rejoice my friend, because God is doing a great work in you right now. *So, In the name of Jesus, I silence the voice of the enemy who would tell you that nothing has happened.*

Jeremiah 33:3 says, *"Call to Me, and I will answer you, and show you great and mighty things, which you do not know."*

Matthew 7:7 says, *"Ask, and it shall be given to you; seek, and you will find; knock, and it will be opened to you."*

Step Three: Announce

Announce. Woo-who! I'm getting excited. Now you get to announce your release to the world. Using your weapon of words is important because they possess power! Proverbs 18:21 teaches that *"Death and life are in the power of the tongue, And those who love it will eat its fruit."* Because your words are creative, whatever you say over yourself will begin to create your reality in the natural. In Genesis 1, the

Bible says *"Then God said..."* several times to show us a clear system that even God used in order to manifest change.

Then verse 31 of the same chapter says, *"Then God saw."* So God *said* something and then He *saw* what He said. Whether you realize it or not, when you speak truth over yourself, you're fulfilling Scripture and producing results. What kinds of results are you producing is the bigger question.

Our having been made in the *"image and likeness of God"* according to Genesis 1:26, requires that we act like God. So we can call into existence those things we want to see in our lives, which fit God's plan for our lives. With that said, let's do some work.

We've read about Tamar, a woman who due to no fault of her own was violated by a man, and left alone to pick up the pieces. She was drastically hurt by someone she trusted. Her offender was only concerned about what he wanted. He never took the time to consider how his actions would affect her. So my questions for you are: How many times has this happened to you, and what are you to do now?

It is probably safe to say that Tamar felt victimized, embarrassed, and alone. She had every reason to feel like a victim because of the offense. What did she do?

Recall a time when you were deeply hurt and list the emotions you were made to feel.

_____
_____
_____
_____
_____
_____

After reviewing your list, decide whether or not you are still wrestling with some of those emotions. If your answer is yes to any of them, why do you think you are still hurting?

_____
_____
_____
_____
_____
_____

What triggers that pain? Is it mentioning of someone's name, a song you hear, a fragrance you smell, or going to certain places? Describe.

_____
_____
_____

_____
_____
_____

Are you ready to be free? Do you believe that you can overcome feeling like a victim? Be honest.

_____
_____
_____
_____
_____

Letting go of the idea that things could've been different is the first step to your freedom. Instead of asking "God, why did this happen to me?", try asking "God, what am I supposed to learn from what happened to me?" These are two very different questions.

In Scripture we learn that *"...and sends rain on the just and the unjust"* (Matthew 5:45). The fact that we are good, hardworking, or compassionate towards others does not automatically exempt us from hardship. Tamar was a good girl, but she found herself in a hard time.

It's when you decide to grow beyond the hard time that determines your label. We discussed labels in the previous chapter. Being called a "victor;" someone who has overcome or defeated an adversary, instead of a "victim;" one who has been attacked, injured or robbed by an adversary, sounds pretty good to me.

You can learn a lot from this passage of Scripture on how to guard yourself from all kinds of predators, whether they are an emotional or a physical.

What lessons did Tamar learn? What lessons have you learned from the experiences you listed?

_____
_____
_____
_____
_____
_____
_____
_____

You must release your offender(s) to the Lord. 1 Peter 5:7, AMP tells us, "...*Casting the whole of your care* [all your anxieties, all your worries, all your concerns, once and for all] *on Him, for He cares for you affectionately and cares about you watchfully."* Although you may not be able to control others reactions towards you; you *can* control how their reactions *affect* you.

Give everything to God. Don't hold on to your pain. Ask God to remove the emotional torment. Matthew 7:7, AMP says, *"Keep on asking and it will be given you; keep on seeking and you will find; keep on knocking* [reverently] *and* [the door] *will be opened to you."* It is a continual process.

Don't listen to the lies of the enemy that God isn't going to deliver you from hurt feelings of neglect and abandonment. Instead, stand firmly on His Word and *"keep asking…keep seeking… and keep knocking…."*

Keep moving toward your breakthrough. Focus on yourself, not your offender. Remind yourself that *you are not a victim. You are a victor through Christ Jesus!* Say this out loud:

> *"Father, in the name of Jesus, I release my offender(s) to you. I relinquish my right to hold on to what was done to me. I give you complete authority of my emotions and my heart. I have full and complete confidence that you are taking care of this situation for me and I thank You for it. Amen!"*

Four Steps to Overcoming the Victim Mindset

1. **Acknowledge that it happened**

    Don't live in a state of denial, pretending these things never took place. Doing so will only hinder your progress. You were hurt, and the reality is you wish it had never happened; but you cannot undo the past. By facing it head on, you can effectively confront the negative chapters of your testimony, and set a new course for a healthy future.

2. **Stop passing the blame!**

    Bad things happen to good people. However, that does not give you permission to build your life based on those bad things. Don't assume everyone is out to get you. If you don't like the way things are, change your actions.

    You may be where you are with the help of others, but you are your own person. You weren't forced to make some of the decisions you have made because you have a free will and you're capable of making your own decisions. Own your part. Admit your mistakes. No one's perfect. List some of mistakes you need to admit making, and of which you need to take ownership?

    _____
    _____
    _____
    _____

_____
_____
_____
_____
_____

3. **Be proactive, not reactive**

   Change your behavior. Instead of reacting when unexpected things happen to you, decide to make better choices to prevent similar things from happening again. Determine ahead of time that you will respond in godly fashion.

   Look back over your life and take notice of things you responded immaturely, or without faith. Then look again over your life and pinpoint the times when you were proactive and well prepared; and note how different the outcomes were. The enemy is constantly sizing us up, always looking for ways to defeat us. Where are your weaknesses? What areas of your life do you need to be proactive about today? Identifying those areas allows you to be better equipped.

_____
_____
_____
_____

_____
_____
_____
_____

4. **Throw away entitlement thinking**

No one owes you anything! Like everyone else, you must earn your place. Be honest with yourself. In what areas have you sought entitlement? (Think about areas where you've believed you were owed something.)

_____
_____
_____
_____
_____

Again, no one owes you anything. The sooner you grasp this concept, the easier your life will be. It doesn't matter how old you get. That statement will never change. Life and its opportunities are gifts. The primary difference between successful people and unsuccessful people, is that one group decided to take advantage of opportunities; while the other sat, wished, and waited for someone to hand them an opportunity.

You can decide today in which category you will be. This book is a gentle nudge in the right direction toward your success. There is a strength inside you that is ready to be released. *Unleash your power!*

Empowerment Scriptures

"But thanks be to God, who gives us the victory through our Lord Jesus Christ" (1 Corinthians 15:57).

Thessalonians 3:3

"But the Lord is faithful, who will establish you and guard you from the evil one" (2 Thessalonians 3:3).

Our Victory Confession

> *I am not a victim; I'm a victor! I have been given power to live in victory. God has not given me the spirit of fear, but of power, love and a sound mind. (2 Timothy 1:7) I don't accept the negative opinions of others as truth concerning me. I have more to offer in this life. I will be everything that God has designed me to be!*

My Journal…

Chapter 3

The Forgiven Woman: I'm Forgiven

Scripture Reference: Luke 7:36-50 (NKJV,)

A Sinful Woman Forgiven

> ³⁶ Then one of the Pharisees asked Him to eat with him. And He went to the Pharisee's house, and sat down to eat. ³⁷ And behold, a woman in the city who was a sinner, when she knew that Jesus sat at the table in the Pharisee's house, brought an alabaster flask of fragrant oil, ³⁸ and stood at His feet behind Him weeping; and she began to wash His feet with her tears, and wiped them with the hair of her head; and she kissed His feet and anointed them with the fragrant oil. ³⁹ Now when the Pharisee who had invited Him saw this, he spoke to himself, saying, "This Man, if He were a prophet, would know who and what manner of woman this is who is touching

Him, for she is a sinner." ⁴⁰ And Jesus answered and said to him, "Simon, I have something to say to you." So he said, "Teacher, say it." ⁴¹ "There was a certain creditor who had two debtors. One owed five hundred denarii, and the other fifty. ⁴² And when they had nothing with which to repay, he freely forgave them both. Tell Me, therefore, which of them will love him more?" ⁴³ Simon answered and said, "I suppose the one whom he forgave more." And He said to him, "You have rightly judged." ⁴⁴ Then He turned to the woman and said to Simon, "Do you see this woman? I entered your house; you gave Me no water for My feet, but she has washed My feet with her tears and wiped them with the hair of her head. ⁴⁵ You gave Me no kiss, but this woman has not ceased to kiss My feet since the time I came in. ⁴⁶ You did not anoint My head with oil, but this woman has anointed My feet with fragrant oil. ⁴⁷ Therefore I say to you, her sins, which are many, are forgiven, for she loved much. But to whom little is forgiven, the same loves little." ⁴⁸ Then He said to her, "Your sins are forgiven." ⁴⁹ And those who sat at the table with Him began to say to themselves, "Who is this who even forgives sins?" ⁵⁰ Then He said to the woman, "Your faith has saved you. Go in peace."

This is an amazing story of the unconditional and non-judgmental love that God has for us. Here we see a woman who is a sinner. She has not yet entered into a relationship with the Lord, but she recognizes who He is and wants to bless Him.

I like the way the Bible sets up this story. (Since we don't know the woman's name, we'll call her *Sister*) Jesus is at a Pharisee's house eating and Sister invites herself to dinner so she can honor the Lord. Nowhere do we read that she either asked if she could come, or that she received an invitation. She didn't care that she didn't know anyone there, or that she didn't have an invitation; she heard about Jesus being at the house and made it a point to be there as well. *She created her moment with the Lord.*

We have to assume this same attitude. Why do we wait for Jesus to find us when it is partly our responsibility to find Him? Isaiah 55:6, NKJV, says we are to *"Seek the Lord while He may be found, Call upon Him while He is near."*

This beautiful woman recognized her responsibility to seek the Lord and she found Him. She accomplished this even as a sinner. (Luke 7:47) Not only did she seek the Lord and create a moment with Him, but she opened a door to allow the Lord to speak well of her. Please understand that your intimate time of prayer and entering the presence of God not only allows you to speak to Him but it opens the line of communication for Him to minister to you. In Isaiah

55:3 the Lord tells us, *"Incline your ear, and come to Me. Hear, and your soul shall live; And I will make an everlasting covenant with you..."*

In the midst of the ridicule directed at her from the religious people, Jesus spoke of her sacrifice and praised her for recognizing who He was. He praised her for washing His feet and anointing His head, which were customary acts of that day, though usually performed by the host. However, not one of the religious leaders, who were supposed to know and execute these customs, offered them to Jesus.

Jesus stopped and took notice of her acts of consideration. Knowing she was a sinner, He looked at her and recognized the good thing she had done. Notice that Jesus never referred to any of her faults. *He was well aware of her past, but He was focused on her future.*

We've made a lot of wrong moves, and God knows them all. One of the great things about God is that He does not see us according to the wrong we've done. He sees us according to those things that are right with us. Jesus knew this woman's past without ever being told, but He chose to speak well of her anyway. It is not the nature of God to highlight our misbehaviors. As stated in Psalm 16:11, NKJV, *"...in the presence of the Lord, there is fullness of joy and pleasures at your right hand forevermore."*

Sister was in the presence of the Lord, so good was the only thing that could emerge. She was not in the presence of another religious person who would condemn her for her past behavior. She was in the presence of the only One who could set her free; the One who would deliver, redeem, and restore her to God's original purpose for her life.

Her previous lifestyle choices had not lined up with the will of God for her life. We know this because verse 37 says, *"...a woman in the city who was a sinner...brought an alabaster flask of fragrant oil..."* She did not fit in with those in attendance at the dinner party. However, her poor reputation did not disqualify her from experiencing God. If anything, her checkered past made her all the more qualified for what Jesus had to offer.

The enemy will try to plant the lie that in order for God to accept you, you have to have it all together. But if you were capable of fixing things yourself, you would not need God at all. Our past mistakes do not remove God's love from us; they draw His love towards us. *"God showed his love towards us, while we were yet sinners..."* (Romans 5:8a)

Once we repent for our sins and accept Christ as our Lord and Savior, our past sins are eradicated. *If any of your past sins are constantly being replayed over and over again in your mind it's not a reminder from the Lord.* It's clearly the enemy's tactic. It's an indication that the enemy wants to keep you in bondage to your past.

In the book of Revelations 12:10, NKJV, we discover that the enemy is referred to as the "accuser of the brethren." This means that once we receive Christ as our Lord, we are now in the family of God, and Satan begins his attempt to discredit us. Satan hates us and does not want us to experience the fullness of what God has to offer. He knows the greatness of God because he once partook of it until he was cast out of heaven for his rebellion. (Revelation 12:9)

By constantly throwing accusing darts our way, he hopes to distract us, and take our focus off of our ultimate goal which is to live out our purpose based on the promises in God's Word.

Here is a woman who is worshipping the Lord from her broken place and people around her are focused on her past. She is presented with two options.

Option #1: She could choose to remain in her brokenness, turn around and leave untouched and unchanged. Had she done so, she would've missed her opportunity to encounter God. Option #2: She could reach for what she'd never had. She could stand in faith, and boldly worship the Lord in spite of the distractions around her.

Of course, we know the choice she made. It was no easy thing. In fact, it was an act of bravery. Everyone in the room knew the life she'd lived. But, she understood that her being in the presence of the King demanded a response.

She stood behind Jesus and began to honor Him by anointing Him with costly perfume, washing His feet with her tears, and drying them with her hair. She blessed Him with what she had. She "loved much," without any expectation of reciprocation. (Luke 7:47) She tuned her heart to worship the Lord.

Real worship will cost you something! Some biblical scholars believe that the costly perfume with which she anointed Jesus was valued at a year's wages. The oil belonged to her, and was intended for her to use on the day she married. Instead of waiting for that day, she chose to offer this precious oil to Jesus. This was an act of great love and appreciation. Sister's actions made the statement "Lord, my love for you is great!" Ask yourself if you are willing to pay the cost?

The key to a successful relationship with God is to recognize the price, and possess the willingness to pay that price. This frame of mind sets you apart from others. It will cost time and energy. This is the difference between one person's *God experience* and another's. One has weighed the cost, and is willing to pay the price. The other has weighed the cost and is unwilling to pay.

God is so good that He allows us to experience the benefits of His grace based on whatever we bring to him. Scripture states *"Give, and it will be given to you: good measure, pressed down, shaken together, and running over will be put into your bosom. For with the same measure that you use, it will be measured back to you"* (Luke 6:38).

What can we learn from the humble stance that this brave woman took? We learn that like Sister, we too are presented with two options in every situation.

Option #1: We can remain the same, and return to our old ways.

Option #2: We can go for what we've never had.

Sister went against what was deemed normal according to popular opinion regarding her life. Maybe other women desired the same experience that she had. But unlike her, they chose Option #1. They stayed where they were. Instead of missing her chance, she stepped out in faith and took action.

She shows us that even at risk of being mocked and ridiculed, it pays to be in the presence of the Lord. Some people may not agree with your decision to move forward. To leave your past and move forward will cause you to leave them behind, and they won't like it. But, at the risk of losing relationships, Sister went to the house anyway. She risked public embarrassment as she pressed into an encounter with God.

For me to decide that my life was going to be Christ-filled and Christ-led wasn't met with favor with some of my then friends and acquaintances. I remember having jokes made about me, and being made the laughingstock because I chose Jesus. When I got saved, *I got saved*! Thinking back on it, I was overzealous and a little too aggressive at times; but I was passionate about the things of God. In the eyes of those people I was no longer fun anymore. I remember being subtly ushered out of a person's house because I talked about Jesus. As much as that hurt me, going back to my old life was not an option. I was done with that. My *new life* with Jesus meant everything to me!

In the presence of her enemies, Sister created an opportunity to enter into the presence of the Lord and it was well worth it. The psalmist tells us in Psalm 23 that he prepares our table "in the presence of our enemies!" Once she was there and aware that she had His attention, she lost sight of those around her.

Here is another great lesson for us to learn from this courageous woman. Never do we read where she acknowledged the words and slanderous statements that were being thrown at her. She didn't try to change the opinions of other people concerning her. *Trying to prove yourself to people will only leave you exhausted and disappointed.*

Even with the eyes of everyone watching you, anticipating your demise, your responsibility is to lock your focus on what matters. People will talk about you, and not everybody will like you. Some will attempt to discourage you from spreading your wings and flying higher. This happens for several reasons.

First, they will do so because they are jealous. Jealousy is birthed out of fear and those who operate in it are afraid that they cannot achieve their own levels of success. Jealousy is also evidence of a poor self-image.

Secondly, they don't know you like God knows you. People who try to discourage and hold you back are relating to the old you and not the new you. They don't understand the powerful transformation that the Gospel of Christ performs. They are not aware that the change has taken place.

Thirdly, they are incapable of encouragement. Some people are "relationally crippled." Sometimes our naysayers only know how to spew out harsh and demeaning comments, because that's all they've ever taken in. And with the help of the Holy Spirit, you will learn how to extend God's grace to individuals who qualify for any one of the three scenarios I've described.

Take Jesus for example. As He was dying on the cross for them, His accusers shouted and mocked Him. But He didn't defend Himself, shout back at them, or call down angels from Heaven to destroy them. Instead, He turned to His Father and prayed for them. (Luke 23:34) By example, Jesus showed us how to pray for those who persecute us. (Matthew 5:44)

Our job is not to respond in the same ill manner, but to speak life over them. Doing this causes us to walk into a new level of spiritual maturity. Matthew 5:48, AMP says, *"You therefore, must be perfect* [growing into complete maturity of godliness in mind and character, having reached the proper height of virtue and integrity], *as your heavenly Father is perfect."* God is a good Daddy. He will never ask something of you; then fail to reward your obedience. Matthew 7:11, NKJV, says, *"If you then, being evil, know how to give good gifts to you children, how much more will your Father who is in heaven give good gifts to those who ask Him!"*

This is important for us to know if we're to live a forgiven life. For you to forgive others is not only for the benefit of your offender. It's also to your benefit. For you to extend forgiveness allows forgiveness to be extended back to you. In Matthew 6:14-15, NKJV, Jesus says, *"For if you forgive men their trespasses, your heavenly Father will also forgive you. But if you don't forgive men their trespasses, neither will your Father forgive your trespasses."*

Take some time right now to *Acknowledge, Ask* and *Announce!* If you're not sure how to do that, then repeat these words.

> "Father, I acknowledge that I have been holding un-forgiveness in my heart towards **[Insert name(s) here]**, and I don't want to hold this any longer. I release the idea of how things could've been, and own the reality of what has

actually happened. Help me walk in forgiveness. I release it all, and hold nothing back for myself to handle. I am no longer bound by bitterness, and anger; nor am I controlled any longer by negative emotions. I thank you for the lessons learned, and the wisdom gained. Thank you for causing this to work for my good.

I declare that I am forgiven, and I walk in and extend forgiveness in Jesus' name, Amen!"

Now that you have asked for God's help, praise Him for doing an awesome work in your life. Thank Him for releasing you to live at a new spiritual level. You've now turned a corner to start experiencing a brand new life.

When those repetitive and negative thoughts come, it's your responsibility to bring those thoughts under subjection to the Word of God. How do you do that? I'm glad you asked.

Recite 2 Corinthians 10:5 which says, *"casting down arguments and every high thing that exalts itself against the knowledge of God, bringing every thought into captivity to the obedience of Christ..."* This Scripture says we're to take authority over every thought that doesn't line up with God's

Word. You may have to do this several times a day, or even multiple times an hour at first.

Don't become weary in well doing. (Galatians 6:9) Be encouraged, God's Word is working. One day you will realize the transformation that's taken place and how your mind has been renewed. (Romans 12:2)

No one knows your past mistakes better than you. But the great thing about God is, once you ask for forgiveness He never brings up your past again. As a matter of fact He said *"As far as the East is from the West, so far has He removed our transgressions from us"* (Psalm 103:12). God will never mention your past. He will only speak life into your future! *"For I know the thoughts I think toward you, says the Lord, thoughts of peace and not of evil, to give you a future and a hope"* (Jeremiah 29:11). To completely move forward we have to be honest, and ask forgiveness for those things we "know" were wrong.

Have you asked God to forgive your sins, (wrong doings)?

_____
_____
_____
_____
_____
_____
_____

If not, why not?

_____
_____
_____
_____
_____

Do you believe that receiving God's forgiveness will change your life? Explain your answer.

_____
_____
_____
_____
_____

Ask for Forgiveness

If you haven't asked God to forgive you and would like to, simply pray, *"Father, I have sinned. I ask you now to forgive me of all of my sins."* I encourage you to find a private place and to name out loud the specific sins you are asking God to forgive, and add them to your prayer. To hear yourself speak these things out loud makes them more real.

(I hope you understand what I'm saying here.) Saying them makes it harder to ignore them. Naming them in the safety of the Lord's presence is an outward expression that says "I'm holding nothing back from you God. You know it all."

"For with the heart one believes unto righteousness, and with the mouth confession is made unto salvation" (Romans 10:10).

How did asking God to forgive you make you feel?
_____
_____
_____
_____
_____
_____

You cannot do anything good enough to be saved, or free from sin. *"For by grace you have been saved through faith, and that not of yourselves; it is the gift of God, not of works, lest anyone should boast"* (Ephesians 2:8-9).

Side Note: The enemy may be telling you right now that what you just said was a joke! If so, he's desperately trying to convince you that you are no different, that you are still the same. Yes, you look the same and nothing about your natural situation has changed. *But you ARE different.*

The Bible says, *"Therefore, if anyone be in Christ, he is a new creation; old things have passed away, behold, all things have become new"* (2 Corinthians 5:17).

Meditate on this Scripture for a minute. Really take some time to think about what God is saying to you.

After meditating on the previous Scripture, what does it mean to you now?

_____
_____
_____
_____
_____
_____

Displaying Forgiveness

1. **You must learn how to forgive, as you have been forgiven.**

   Matthew 6:12 tells us, *"...and forgive us our trespasses [sins] as we forgive those who trespass [sin] against us."* As imitators of God (Ephesians 5:1), we are to offer unconditional forgiveness, just as He so graciously extended it to us.

Benefits of God's Forgiveness Include…

- *Freedom.* Christ has made you free. (Galatians 5:1)
- *Undeserved.* We are not worthy of the grace He's bestowed upon us by loving us, forgiving us, and providing a way of escape from our sin. "*[All] are justified and made upright and in right standing with God, freely and gratuitously by His grace (His unmerited favor and mercy), through the redemption which is [provided] in Christ Jesus…*" Romans 3:23-24
- *Access to Eternal Life.* "*…that whoever believes in him shall not perish but have eternal life*" (John 3:16, NIV)
- *Released from bondage.* "*…and do not be entangled again with a yoke of bondage…*" (Galatians 5:1).

2. **Apply these benefits of forgiveness to your life**

   Forgiveness severs the tie between you and your past, so you can be free to experience all that God has for you. Extending forgiveness to those who've sinned against you, puts you in position to receive God's forgiveness for your sins. (Matthew 6:12)

Walking in forgiveness

The idea of forgiveness can be a scary thing for some because it is perceived that in order to forgive; you must excuse the wrong that was done to you. If you forgive, you are telling the other person that what they did was okay. *This is NOT what forgiveness is.*

To forgive is to say, "I renounce, give up, and reject anger or resentment against the person who's hurt me." Forgiveness is not only for the one you forgive. Forgiveness is *for you*! How is this possible?

Well, holding on to the wrong that someone has done to you holds you in that place of hurt. It robs you of the freedom to move forward, or to move beyond that hurt. For you to harbor anger causes you to rehearse every negative thing they've done to you, which never allows your wounds to heal. So, instead of using the unfortunate incident to help you grow into a wiser woman, you remain bitter and your spiritual growth is stunted. To forgive is a beautiful decision. Expose the beauty within this gift.

List the names of the people you need to forgive and for what.

_____
_____
_____
_____
_____
_____

Now, simply ask God to help you start the healing process and help you forgive them.

SN: Do this with the understanding that you may never hear "I'm sorry", but you are walking in forgiveness anyway.

Empowerment Scriptures

"For if you forgive men their trespasses, your heavenly Father will also forgive you. But if you do not forgive men their trespasses, neither will your Father forgive your trespasses" (Matthew 6:14-15).

"Then Peter came to Him and said, "Lord, how often shall my brother sin against me, and I forgive him? Up to seven times?" 22 Jesus said to him, "I do not say to you, up to seven times, but up to seventy times seven. 23 Therefore the kingdom of heaven is like a certain king who wanted to settle accounts with his servants. 24 And when he had begun to settle accounts, one was brought to him who owed him ten thousand talents. 25 But as he was not able to pay, his master commanded that he be sold, with his wife and children and all that he had, and that payment be made. 26 The servant therefore fell down before him, saying, 'Master, have

patience with me, and I will pay you all.' ²⁷ *Then the master of that servant was moved with compassion, released him, and forgave him the debt.* ²⁸ *"But that servant went out and found one of his fellow servants who owed him a hundred denarii; and he laid hands on him and took him by the throat, saying, 'Pay me what you owe!'* ²⁹ *So his fellow servant fell down at his feet and begged him, saying, 'Have patience with me, and I will pay you all.'* ³⁰ *And he would not, but went and threw him into prison till he should pay the debt.* ³¹ *So when his fellow servants saw what had been done, they were very grieved, and came and told their master all that had been done.* ³² *Then his master, after he had called him, said to him, 'You wicked servant! I forgave you all that debt because you begged me.* ³³ *Should you not also have had compassion on your fellow servant, just as I had pity on you?'* ³⁴ *And his master was angry, and delivered him to the torturers until he should pay all that was due to him.*³⁵ *"So My heavenly Father also will do to you if each of you, from his heart, does not forgive his brother his trespasses"* (Matthew 18:21-35).

Prayer of Forgiveness

Lord, I don't want to forgive **[Insert name(s) here]**. I have been hurt far above what I can even express with words. So I'm asking for Your help! Help me to understand that forgiveness is for me and not for them. Help me to forgive like you forgave me. Today I choose to walk in forgiveness towards all those who have hurt me, with You leading the way.

My Journal...

Chapter 4

Gomer: My Past is NOT My Future

Scripture Reference: Hosea 1:2-3, NKJV

The Family of Hosea

> When the LORD began to speak by Hosea, the LORD said to Hosea:
>
> 'Go, take yourself a wife of harlotry And children of harlotry, For the land has committed great harlotry *By departing* from the LORD.' ³So he went and took Gomer the daughter of Diblaim, and she conceived and bore him a son."

Leaving your past and walking into your future is the easy part. It is making the decision to leave your past and walk into your future that is hard. All change takes time to adapt to. After doing something one way for so long, and having that routine altered, can be a shock to the system. However, that doesn't give us license to not create new norms by which to live. This idea is what Gomer struggled with.

The name *Gomer* means "a sudden stop" or "a termination." (http://tinyurl.com/l6kypmt) I find that interesting. In this passage of Scripture, that depicts Gomer very well.

God had sent Hosea to redeem Gomer who seems determined to be difficult and to cling to her past. She keeps reverting to her old way of life. God sent her a man who was assigned to love, protect, and nurture her back to a place of health. But instead of embracing the care that was being extended to her, Gomer suddenly walked away from it. She terminated it and returned to her previous lifestyle.

It only *seems* sudden. You see, this wasn't an overnight reversal. No, this reversal came after years of having experienced God's love and grace. She had started a family and had experienced the unconditional love of her husband. But there was still part of her that longed for what she once knew.

This behavior comes from a lack of total surrender. Before we get into that let's review what we've learned so far.

In Chapter 1 we discovered that our self-esteem is not tied to anyone's acceptance of us. Since we are learning about Gomer we see this is quite evident in her case because Hosea took her as his wife, and cared for her while something was still missing in her.

In Chapter 2 we learned that bad things happen to good people, and we possess the power and ability to move on and not live in the past. Matthew 5:45 says, *"…that you may be sons of your Father in heaven; for He makes His sun rise on the evil and on the good, and sends rain on the just and on the unjust."*

But we are reassured by Psalm 34:19 that *"Many are the afflictions of the righteous, But the Lord delivers him out of them all."*

In Chapter 3 we acknowledged the reality of our past hurts and asked God to help us release them. Then we announced our freedom to enter our God-ordained future.

All of what we have reviewed is great, but we must be careful. Although the Bible does not tell us the steps Gomer took to become the wife and mother she was in this season of her life, it's not a far stretch to think she might have taken some of those same steps.

She may have dealt with the lack of self-esteem along with trying to move forward, away from the bad choices she'd made. She may have tried to acknowledge her past hurts, and attempted to walk in forgiveness. But if we don't totally surrender *all of it* to the Lord, we will find ourselves still struggling with old behavioral patterns.

It's vitally important at this stage in your growth process that you give to God all the things that you *don't* talk about, those secrets you try to *hide* from Him and from yourself. Those are the ones that the enemy uses to keep you feeling condemned. To condemn, by definition, means "to express strong disapproval; to judge or declare to be unfit for use." (www.thefreedictionary.com). Accusing us to be unfit is the enemy's plan. Revelation 12:10 *"…for the accuser of our brethren, who accused them before our God day and night…"* He wants us to believe that we are not of any use to God and that nothing good can come from us. When we allow ourselves to withhold information from God and try to work it out on our own, that's an opportunity for Satan to accuse us. Once that begins, guilt sets in and we convince ourselves that God is mad at us and we hide from Him. Genesis 3:8 *"And they heard the sound of the Lord God walking in the garden in the cool of the day, and Adam and his wife hid themselves from the presence of the Lord God among the trees of the garden."* Adam and Eve hid themselves from the presence of God because they bought into the lie of the enemy which is a response that man is still operating in today.

We have access to the throne of God that Satan no longer has and he hates us because of it. That we can *"come *boldly to the throne of grace,"* according to Hebrews 4:16, should make us run quickly to repentance!

Here's the balance with this. No, you are NOT perfect. You *will* make mistakes. But God already knows that and He chose you anyway! (Romans 5:8, NKJV) He knows the end from the beginning, (Isaiah 46:9-10) and already He knows the mistakes we will make and how many times we will make them. But the Bible says *"For a righteous man may fall seven times and rise again..."* (Proverbs 24:16, NKJV). My pastor, James K. Hart of Eagle's Nest Worship Center, in Omaha, NE says it this ways *"Failure isn't in falling, failure is in staying down".*

Out of every mistake we should learn a lesson. If we are not learning from our mistakes, we have to question if we are truly submitted to God's plan. Don't repeat your mistakes again and again. Instead, allow yourself to grow because of them. God is merciful. Psalm 59:17, NKJV, *"To You, O my Strength, I will sing praises; For God is my defense, My God of mercy."* He is not looking to destroy you for your mistakes. He's waiting to pick you back up and help you move forward.

Despite Gomer's background from which she'd emerged, God still called her to be the wife of that young preacher, Hosea. There was much more purpose left in Gomer yet to be revealed. Even after all of her deliberate acts of running away from his unconditional love, and walking back into sin, Hosea still loved Gomer intensely! What a great example of God's unending, unfailing and undying love for us. To completely let go of your past is scary to say the least, because it has defined your life for so long. However, the benefits of that release are far more rewarding than remaining bound. God doesn't care how many times you miss it, *He wants <u>you</u>*!

The Bible says that Hosea paid a price for his bride, Gomer, who had reverted to her former ways. But to reclaim what belonged to him, he sought her out, found her, and loved her right in the midst of her mess! That is what God does for us. Even when we don't live like it, He still loves us. *Never forget, God can transform our messes into His messages!*

No one knows you better than you do, and you know what you can and cannot keep on this journey. Make a list of those things you know you must get rid of to prevent you from making a wrong choice.

_____
_____
_____
_____
_____

What type of love did Hosea express towards Gomer?

_____
_____
_____
_____
_____

When Hosea took Gomer back, he spoke to her future not to her past. In Judges 6:11, we read about Gideon, who was hiding in the winepress from the enemy. While he was there he encountered the Angel of the Lord, and there the Lord calls Gideon a "mighty man of valor."

This is another awesome picture of God's love towards us. He never sees us according to our past, or even our current fleshly condition. He only speaks to us in terms of who we are in Him, and our future selves in Christ.

How can you prevent yourself from staying in, or going back to familiar situations, even when the unfamiliar is scary?

_____
_____
_____
_____
_____

_____
_____
_____
_____
_____

Empowerment Scriptures

"Therefore, if anyone is in Christ, he is a new creation; old things have passed away; behold, all things have become new"
(2 Corinthians 5:17).

"And no one puts new wine into old wineskins; or else the new wine bursts the wineskins, the wine is spilled, and the wineskins are ruined. But new wine must be put into new wineskins" (Matthew 9:17).

Confession over My Present and My Future

From this day forward, I decree and declare that I no longer look to my past to determine who I am now, or in the future. I am fully persuaded that nothing can separate me from the love of God. I am victorious! I am virtuous! I am confident! My future is full of great things prepared for me by my

Father. I have been granted access into the rooms of the Kingdom of God. I am fearfully and wonderfully made. I am God's woman!

My Journal...

Chapter 5

The Accused Woman: Don't Rehearse Your Mistakes

Scripture Reference: John 8:1-11, NKJV

But Jesus went to the Mount of Olives. ² Now early in the morning He came again into the temple, and all the people came to Him; and He sat down and taught them. ³ Then the scribes and Pharisees brought to Him a woman caught in adultery. And when they had set her in the midst, ⁴ they said to Him, "Teacher, this woman was caught in adultery, in the very act. ⁵ Now Moses, in the law, commanded us that such should be stoned. But what do You say?" ⁶ This they said, testing Him, that they might have something of which to accuse Him. But Jesus stooped down and wrote on the ground with His finger, as though He did not hear. ⁷ So when they continued asking Him, He raised

Himself up and said to them, "He who is without sin among you, let him throw a stone at her first." ⁸ And again He stooped down and wrote on the ground. ⁹ Then those who heard it, being convicted by their conscience, went out one by one, beginning with the oldest even to the last. And Jesus was left alone, and the woman standing in the midst. ¹⁰ When Jesus had raised Himself up and saw no one but the woman, He said to her, "Woman, where are those accusers of yours? Has no one condemned you?" ¹¹ She said, "No one, Lord." And Jesus said to her, "Neither do I condemn you; go and sin no more."

How great is God! This Bible story brings me so much peace when my mind starts to replay some of the horrible mistakes I've made. When reading this passage I begin to imagine Jesus standing between me and my accusers, guarding and protecting me regardless of what I've done.

I have encountered some extremely embarrassing moments in my life that have caused me to live with some heavy consequences, but as He told the accused woman, Jesus told me *"I do not condemn you…"* John 8:11, AMP.

God is no respecter of persons. (Acts 10:34, KJV) He won't make a promise to one child and not offer the same promise to another child. His promises are available to all of

His children, but it us up to each child to accept them. Once we receive Him, we receive everything that comes with Him. 2 Corinthians 1:20 says, *"For all the promises of God in Him are Yes and in Him Amen...,"* which means that all the promises are mine because He is mine. One promise He made to us which is the one He so graciously exhibited to the woman in our story is found in Psalm 103:12. *"As far as the east is from the west, So far has He removed our transgressions from us."*

I am so grateful that I serve a God who forgives all my sins when I sincerely repent. Acts 3:19 reads, *"Repent therefore and be converted, that your sins may be blotted out, so that times of refreshing may come from the presence of the Lord..."*

Thank You Lord! I can certainly attest to needing refreshment after I've had a huge mess up. To be refreshed means to be given new strength or energy; to reinvigorate. (www.oxforddictionaries.com) Once you ask your Father to forgive you, there is a new supernatural life that is released to you. Natural words can't fully express the peace, the joy, and the relief that overwhelms you when you've repented.

Repentance means to have a change of mind about sin and about God, which results in turning from sin and turning to God. When we repent we are saying that our attitude towards sin mirrors or reflects God's attitude towards sin. We've decided to look at things God's way.

In Deuteronomy 30:19 the Lord tells us, *"...that I have set before you life and death, blessing and cursing; therefore choose life, that both you and your descendants may live..."* Our decision to do things God's way, leads us to life and blessing. It's a Kingdom promise! Matthew 6:33 says it this way. *"But seek first the kingdom of God and His righteousness, and all these things shall be added to you."* God's methods always produce benefits and rewards.

In our limited natural thinking we reason ourselves out of receiving all the great and awesome promises that God has for us. We assume that our mistakes and mess-ups are far too great for God to forgive. Remember in Chapter 1 I said that being human means that any fix we try in our own power will be flawed; however, God's power is perfect and complete! As long as we allow ourselves to live under that umbrella of shame and guilt, we will miss all the great things He has in store for us.

This thinking results from our lack of understanding the true nature and character of God. We will never be able to fully comprehend the character of God. He is too great. But there are certain qualities of which we can be certain.

One of which is; God is our Father. 2 Corinthians 6:18 says, *"I will be a Father to you, And you shall be My sons and daughters, Says the Lord Almighty."* This was His declaration to us. In Psalm 8:4 the angels in heaven asked, *"What is man that You are mindful of him, And the son of man that You visit him?"* Even the angels took notice of God's love and compassion for us. They were astonished that He would think about us and grace us with His ability and His presence.

As a parent I understand the kind of unconditional love God has for His children. My husband and I have been blessed with four beautiful children. Each of them has an equal place in our hearts. We don't love one more than the other. Any of them have access to us at any time, and are given our full attention when they need it. We give the very best that we have to our children without them asking for it.

In Matthew 7:11 we read, *"If you then, being evil, know how to give good gifts to your children, how much more will your Father who is in heaven give good things to those who ask Him!"* He's always waiting to extend the very best of Himself to us. Your Father desires for you to reap the benefits of living your life in fellowship with Him.

The woman in our story was dragged into the presence of Jesus; a Man she had undoubtedly heard about. He is the same man who was doing great and mighty miracles for different people. She was being accused in His presence. She's thrown in front of Him because of sinful acts she has committed, not because of things that have been done to her. *She's guilty.* She willingly acted out.

Okay! Hold up! Can you imagine that level of embarrassment? Here stands the Savior of the world right in front of you and He knows what you did. Oh my goodness! But, instead of ridicule and harsh words, Jesus responds according to James 3:17, *"But the wisdom from above is first pure, then peaceable, gentle, open to reason, full of mercy and good fruits, impartial and sincere."*

A great sense of relief and peace must have consumed this young woman as she stood there alone, free of her accusers and alive! Jesus told her, *"Go and sin no more."*

After I returned home from dropping out of college, pregnant and alone, I had to face many accusers as well. I remember walking around with what seemed like a coat of guilt and shame.

Every morning I woke up and wrapped myself in guilt and shame like I would an article of clothing. I was angry at myself and constantly beat myself up for the disappointment I'd caused everybody else. This became an everyday cycle. I couldn't shake it.

I remember many nights, lying in bed crying and telling myself that my life was over. I had no motivation and absolutely no vision or hope for the future. I believed that I was a horrible person. I gradually embraced every negative word that was ever spoken to me, or about me. This was my daily routine for five months.

One Sunday morning I was sitting in church looking sad and pitiful, when an elderly woman I called "Grandma

Moses" walked over to me. She said something to me that changed my life!

She hugged me and she said "Sweetie, you only have to ask one Person to forgive you and you only have to ask Him once." Those words set me free! I spent the rest of the day rehearsing her words over and over and over again.

That night, I prayed like I've never prayed before. I called out to God and I knew He heard me. I repented knowing that He forgave me. The next day I woke up and I felt different. The garments of guilt and shame were no longer part of my wardrobe. I got dressed and presented myself to the world as a free woman.

I was able to smile again, and look people in the eye. I was free to enjoy the blessing of being the mom to one of the most beautiful babies ever to grace this earth. It wasn't the denial that I had not made a mistake but it was the comfort of knowing that He loved me, and still called me His, in spite of my mistake.

There were still some people who wanted to rehearse my mistakes, but it didn't matter because by then, *I absolutely knew who I was*. I was His and He was mine. He didn't condemn me, so I didn't need to condemn myself. With my eyes locked in on Him, He began to reveal to me portions of my purpose and destiny. Jeremiah 29:11 became a reality in my life. *"For I know the thoughts that I think toward you, says the Lord, thoughts of peace and not of evil, to give you a future and a hope."* My hope was restored and my faith renewed. My life wasn't over. I wasn't a horrible person. God still loved me!

Today, I speak the same thing to you that was spoken to me that day. You only have to ask one Person for forgiveness, and you only have to ask Him once. Since the moment I heard those words, my life has never been the same. I pray that those words bring you as much comfort as they did for me that Sunday, morning 14 years ago.

In this powerful passage of Scripture we see Jesus teaching in the temple. And while He was teaching, the Scribes and Pharisees (religious, non-relational people) brought him a woman they'd caught in adultery. Interestingly, none of her accusers addressed the absence of the man whom she had committed adultery with.

Not only did she suffer the indignity of having been dragged through the streets, but they brought her to Jesus! They were ready to stone her for an act she obviously could not have committed by herself.

Once again, Jesus displayed His unfailing love and compassion. He spoke to her and forgave her without even once addressing her sin. He simply reassured her that she was not the only one dealing with imperfection.

Describe a time when you felt embarrassed or humiliated. What effect did that have on you?

_____
_____
_____
_____
_____
_____

Feelings of embarrassment and humiliation are real, however, you don't have to live there. What are some ways that you can begin to release those feelings? *(Here is one suggestion: start a journal, writing is an excellent release of emotions or even start a video journal. Get it out, don't hold on to it.)*

_____
_____
_____
_____
_____
_____

This change can be immediate. That's so exciting. How long does it take for you to change your direction?

_____
_____
_____
_____
_____
_____

List some ways that will keep you headed in the right Godly direction.

1. _____
2. _____
3. _____
4. _____
5. _____
6. _____

Empowerment Scriptures

"Yet in all these things we are more than conquerors through Him who loved us" (Romans 8:37).

"Now thanks be to God who always leads us in triumph in Christ, and through us diffuses the fragrance of His knowledge in every place" (2 Corinthians 2:14.

Prayer over my Future

Heavenly Father I thank you for now giving me the ability to see myself the way you see me. I decree that I have no cares because I have cast them all on you, Father, because you care for me. My future is sealed by the blood of your sinless Son, Jesus. I will not allow in any negative influence to shape and mold my character or my behavior. In all my ways I acknowledge you. You are directing my path. In Jesus' name, Amen!

My Journal...

_____
_____
_____
_____
_____
_____
_____

Chapter 6

Ruth: Moving Forward

Scripture Reference: The Book of Ruth, NKJV

Ruth 1

Elimelech's Family Goes to Moab

Now it came to pass, in the days when the judges ruled, that there was a famine in the land. And a certain man of Bethlehem, Judah, went to dwell in the country of Moab, he and his wife and his two sons. ² The name of the man was Elimelech, the name of his wife was Naomi, and the names of his two sons were Mahlon and Chilion—Ephrathites of Bethlehem, Judah. And they went to the country of Moab and remained there. ³ Then Elimelech, Naomi's husband, died; and she was left, and her two sons. ⁴ Now they took wives of the women of Moab: the name of the one was Orpah, and the name of the other Ruth. And they dwelt there about ten years. ⁵ Then both Mahlon and Chilion also died; so the woman survived her two sons and her husband.

Naomi Returns with Ruth

⁶ Then she arose with her daughters-in-law that she might return from the country of Moab, for she had heard in the country of Moab that the LORD had visited His people by giving them bread. ⁷ Therefore she went out from the place where she was, and her two daughters-in-law with her; and they went on the way to return to the land of Judah. ⁸ And Naomi said to her two daughters-in-law, "Go, return each to her mother's house. The LORD deal kindly with you, as you have dealt with the dead and with me. ⁹ The LORD grant that you may find rest, each in the house of her husband." So she kissed them, and they lifted up their voices and wept. ¹⁰ And they said to her, "Surely we will return with you to your people." ¹¹ But Naomi said, "Turn back, my daughters; why will you go with me? Are there still sons in my womb, that they may be your husbands? ¹² Turn back, my daughters, go—for I am too old to have a husband. If I should say I have hope, if I should have a husband tonight and should also bear sons, ¹³ would you wait for them till they were grown? Would you restrain yourselves from having husbands? No, my daughters; for it grieves me very much for your sakes that the hand of the LORD has gone out against me!" ¹⁴ Then they lifted up their voices and wept again; and Orpah kissed her mother-in-law, but Ruth clung to her. ¹⁵ And she said, "Look, your sister-in-law has gone back to her people and to her gods; return after your sister-in-law." ¹⁶ But Ruth said: "Entreat me not to leave you, Or to turn back from following after you; For wherever you go, I will go; And wherever you lodge, I will lodge; Your people shall be my people, And your God, my God. ¹⁷ Where you die, I will die, And there will I be buried. The LORD do so to me, and more also, If anything but death parts you and me." ¹⁸ When she saw that she was determined to go with her, she stopped speaking to her. ¹⁹ Now the two of them went until they came to Bethlehem. And it happened, when they had come to Bethlehem, that all the city was excited because of them; and the women said, "Is this Naomi?" ²⁰ But she said to them, "Do not call me Naomi;[a] call me Mara,[b] for the Almighty has dealt very bitterly with me. ²¹ I went out full, and the LORD has brought me home again empty. Why do you call me Naomi, since the LORD has testified against me, and the Almighty has afflicted me?" ²² So Naomi returned, and Ruth *the Moabitess her daughter-in-law with her, who returned from the country of Moab. Now they came to Bethlehem at the beginning of barley harvest.*

Ruth 4

Boaz Redeems Ruth

Now Boaz went up to the gate and sat down there; and behold, the close relative of whom Boaz had spoken came by. So Boaz said, "Come aside, friend, sit down here." So he came aside and sat down. ² And he took ten men of the elders of the city, and said, "Sit down here." So they sat down. ³ Then he said to the close relative, "Naomi, who has come back from the country of Moab, sold the piece of land which belonged to our brother Elimelech. ⁴ And I thought to inform you, saying, 'Buy it back in the presence of the inhabitants and the elders of my people. If you will redeem it, redeem it; but if you will not redeem it, then tell me, that I may know; for there is no one but you to redeem it, and I am next after you.'" And he said, "I will redeem it." ⁵ Then Boaz said, "On the day you buy the field from the hand of Naomi, you must also buy it from Ruth the Moabitess, the wife of the dead, to perpetuate the name of the dead through his inheritance." ⁶ And the close relative said, "I cannot redeem it for myself, lest I ruin my own inheritance. You redeem my right of redemption for yourself, for I cannot redeem it." ⁷ *Now this was the custom in former times in Israel concerning redeeming and exchanging, to confirm anything: one man took off his sandal and gave it to the other, and this was a confirmation in Israel.* ⁸ *Therefore the close relative said to Boaz, "Buy it for yourself." So he took off his sandal.* ⁹ *And Boaz said to the elders and all the people, "You are witnesses this day that I have bought all that was Elimelech's, and all that was Chilion's and Mahlon's, from the hand of Naomi.* ¹⁰ *Moreover, Ruth the Moabitess, the widow of Mahlon, I have acquired as my wife, to perpetuate the name of the dead through his inheritance, that the name of the dead may not be cut off from among his brethren and from his position at the gate. You are witnesses this day."* ¹¹ *And all the people who were at the gate, and the elders, said, "We are witnesses. The* LORD *make the woman who is coming to your house like Rachel and Leah, the two who built the house of Israel; and may you prosper in Ephrathah and be famous in Bethlehem.* ¹² *May your house be like the house of Perez, whom Tamar bore to Judah, because of the offspring which the* LORD *will give you from this young woman."*

Descendants of Boaz and Ruth

¹³ So Boaz took Ruth and she became his wife; and when he went in to her, the LORD gave her conception, and she bore a son. ¹⁴ Then the women said to Naomi, "Blessed be the LORD, who has not left you this day without a close relative; and may his name be famous in Israel! ¹⁵ And may he be to you a restorer of life and a nourisher of your old age; for your daughter-in-law, who loves you, who is better to you than seven sons, has borne him." ¹⁶ Then Naomi took the child and laid him on her bosom, and became a nurse to him. ¹⁷ Also the neighbor women gave him a name, saying, "There is a son born to Naomi." And they called his name Obed. He is the father of Jesse, the father of David.

"Boaz married Ruth. She became his wife." (Ruth 4:13, MSG) Those two statements are two statements most women dream about and pray for! For most of us, as little girls we dream of the day we will get married and can't wait to be a wife. We imagine the colors we will use in our wedding, and how many bridesmaids we will have. We have the day planned all the way down to the color of ribbon used on the souvenir bags at the reception.

If you weren't dreaming about your wedding, maybe you were dreaming of the college you would attend to help jumpstart your career with just as much detail. Or perhaps you imagined all the places you would travel to before settling down. However, in all of our planning we never stop to think about the detours life will inevitably cause us to take before we reach our destination. *Life's detours are often God's destiny highways.*

Ruth is a young widow who finds herself in her hometown living with her mother-in-law and sister-in-law. Her husband has died and now the future that she once thought she was preparing for has diminished into the background. She faces some serious life-changing decisions.

Right now as you read this book, you too have a decision to make. After you finishing the book you can put it down and say, "That was a good book;" or you can take the steps that the Holy Spirit is directing you to take to start the process of change. Ruth had a decision to make.

In Ruth 1:6 Naomi, Ruth's mother-in-law, decided to return to her hometown. Ruth along with Orpah, her sister-in-law, decided to follow her. What courage they exemplified. They are leaving the only home they've ever known to follow someone to a place they have never been. That's faith pushed to the limits. Even in the face of fear they begin their travels with Naomi.

Now here's where a lot of us stop. We know that there is something that is great down the road, and it's going to be good, but we're afraid to step out on faith and do it. We end up talking ourselves out of something great before we even start. If we focus on the fear too long we will never get anywhere. I heard fear described as "**F**-alse **E**-vidence **A**-ppearing **R**-eal." The majority of the time the fear we face is mostly produced by the "what if's" we create in our minds.

The thought of the "what if's" weighed heavy on Orpah, who decided she would turn around partway to Judah, and go back home to Moab; but not Ruth. Ruth was determined to see what awaited her.

Right now I want you to do some action steps. *Acknowledge* what you want to see happen in your life. Make a list of all the dreams you've had and want to see manifest.

After you acknowledge what you want, *ask* God to show you where to start. You may not get the answer right away and that's okay. Thank Him in advance, knowing with all assurance that He already has the answer. Then, *announce* to your future that from this day forward you are walking toward your God-ordained destiny and purpose.

In this process you have to avoid what I call the "Orpah Syndrome." We've all experienced this disorder. We start something and halfway through it we talk ourselves right on out of it. And all we are left with is an unfinished project or an unrealized dream. Begrudgingly we're left looking at another "something" we did not follow through on which leads to guilt, embarrassment, envy and even jealousy. It's a horrible sickness. Please, stay away and exercise caution! The Orpah Syndrome is highly contagious. People who have been affected by it don't realize the effect it has on their lives and they will contaminate your life if you are not careful.

Ruth avoided this syndrome. I believe that there were dreams that Ruth wanted to see fulfilled that hadn't yet been fulfilled. She knew she would never see them come to past if she stayed in Moab. Ruth was willing to reach beyond what she could see in the natural toward what she could see in the spirit.

Ruth made a right connection with Naomi. Here's an awesome example of being connected to the right people. Ruth vowed to follow Naomi and be her family always. She was all too aware that her future was in Judah, and not in Moab.

Uh-oh...there's that word again. Judah which we learned in Chapter 1 translates to praise. Like Leah, Ruth found her new identity in the place of praise. Your connections will either draw you closer to praise or further from praise.

Ask yourself, *who am I connected to?* Really reflect on that for a few minutes by answering the following questions.

- Are the people in your life life-givers or life-takers?

- Do you feel better or worse after being around them?

- Do they possess a positive attitude?

- Are their words helpful and hope-full, or hurtful?

Naomi was a life-giver to Ruth. She instructed Ruth with wisdom and kind words to preserve her future. Naomi could've easily given into the sorrow and bitterness she had experienced earlier, but she chose to be gentle and gracious toward Ruth. She didn't take the frustrations in her life out on Ruth.

This is the type of person you need to be connected with. Get connected to someone who will speak life to you even when they may not be experiencing the greatest moments in their own life. This is an extremely important part of your journey. Hook up with people who have been where you are trying to go.

Naomi already knew how to maneuver in Judah and that's where Ruth wanted to be. Because Ruth chose to stay connected with Naomi, great favor was released to her. She caught the attention of the field owner of where she was working. Protection was granted to her along with access to the whole field as if she were one of the ladies of the house.

This kind of favor was granted to her because of her commitment to and the honor she'd shown to Naomi. It matters to whom you commit yourself. Your associations speak a lot about who you are as a person and where you are headed in life. People may not know much about you, but they may know more about the person or people with which you associate.

Ruth's character preceded her. Boaz was impressed by the loyalty and care she exhibited towards her mother-in-law and decided to show her care in return. This was the beginning of a brand new life for Ruth.

In order to truly move forward, you have to take inventory of the associations you have created. This is another hard decision you have to make but you don't have to make it alone. James 1:5 says, *"if any of you lacks wisdom, let him ask of God, who gives to all liberally and without reproach, and it will be given to him."*

Some relationships need to be totally removed, and others need to be altered. Whatever the result, allow the Holy Spirit to show you how to do it. 1 Corinthians 15:33 states, *"Do not be deceived: Evil company corrupts good habits."*

One thing we can count on in life is change. Change is good! Some of us fight change because we enjoy the comfort, and the feeling of security we sense when things remain the same. However, without change we don't grow, and we will never fully see what we were capable of becoming.

Ruth's world changed dramatically. Not only had she lost her husband, she'd chosen to leave the only place she ever lived to travel to a place she'd never been. In the process she lost her sister-in-law, who was part of her everyday life up until that point. She was now faced with living in a place where she was a foreigner and knew only one person in the entire city. But God! God had a greater plan.

God always planned for Ruth to be the great-grandmother of a giant killer, a man after God's own heart—King David. She is in the lineage of Jesus all because of one decision to move forward against all odds.

I want to share some words of a song I wrote that I believe will speak into your life and help you to start your new journey.

> *There's a voice that's speaking soft and sweet to you, sharing a truth that is certain and real.*
>
> *It's revealing grander views of brighter days ahead, a future filled with plans. Your time is in His hands.*
>
> *So close your eyes and listen to His words. Hang all your hopes and dreams on what you've heard. It's your destiny.*
>
> *He's revealing possibilities you never knew were available to you. It's your destiny.*
>
> *Pictures of grand opportunities take hold, and watch your destiny unfold!*

Ruth is a perfect example of what it means to move forward. Ruth was determined to get something she never had before.

Why do you think Ruth decided to continue the journey?

_____
_____
_____
_____
_____
_____

Determine what connections you'll need to get you to your next destination. Write them down and ask God for strategy to see them come to pass.

_____
_____
_____
_____
_____
_____

What characteristics must you possess to move forward even when you're faced with the unknown?

1. _____
2. _____
3. _____
4. _____
5. _____
6. _____

How are you going to move forward starting today?

_____
_____
_____
_____
_____
_____

Empowerment Scriptures

> "But Ruth said: 'Entreat me not to leave you, Or to turn back from following after you; For wherever you go, I will go; And wherever you lodge, I will lodge; Your people shall be my people, And your

God, my God. ⁱ⁷ Where you die, I will die, And there will I be buried. The LORD do so to me, and more also, If anything but death parts you and me'" (Ruth 1:16-17).

Moving Forward Confession

Today, I confess that I will move forward! Because you, Lord, are my light and my salvation, I will not fear. You have made all my crooked places straight and have set me on a path full of success. All of my needs are met. I am abundantly supplied! I press toward the mark of the high calling in Christ Jesus!

My Journal...

_____
_____
_____
_____
_____
_____
_____
_____
_____

Change...

Change has occurred. You should be proud of yourself for taking action to transform your today to unveil a better tomorrow. You are phenomenal!

You have abandoned all excuses. You have taken the cover off of those things Satan tried to keep hidden in darkness, so he could use them against you. You have exposed them to the light of the Son of God!

It's not over. This is only the beginning, but what an awesome start! The fullness of what God has in store for you hasn't even begun to be revealed.

Get ready for great and powerful things to manifest in your life.

On your mark, get set, continue to GROW!

Contact:

**TaRae Peoples Ministries
PO Box 343
Boys Town, NE 68010
info@TaRaePeoplesMinistries.org**

www.ingramcontent.com/pod-product-compliance
Lightning Source LLC
Chambersburg PA
CBHW070626300426
44113CB00010B/1683